THE HOW AND THE WHY

BY SARAH TREEM

★

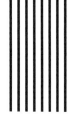

★

DRAMATISTS
PLAY SERVICE
INC.

THE HOW AND THE WHY
Copyright © 2013, Sarah Treem

All Rights Reserved

THE HOW AND THE WHY received its world premiere at the McCarter Theatre Center (Emily Mann, Artistic Director; Timothy J. Shields, Managing Director; Mara Isaacs, Producing Director) in Princeton, New Jersey, opening on January 14, 2011. It was directed by Emily Mann; the set design was by Daniel Ostling; the costume design was by Jennifer Moeller; the lighting design was by Stephen Strawbridge; and the sound design was by Robert Kaplowitz. The cast was as follows:

ZELDA KAHN . . . . Mercedes Ruehl
RACHEL HARDEMAN . . . . Bess Rous

CHARACTERS

ZELDA KAHN, 56
RACHEL HARDEMAN, 28

PLACE

A senior professor's office in Cambridge, Mass.
Later, a dive bar in Boston.

TIME

Present. Late Autumn.

NOTE

These women think and speak quickly. Respect their silences.

THE HOW AND THE WHY

Scene 1

Zelda is behind an elegant mahogany desk, pouring over an unbound manuscript and checking it against a few heavy tomes open before her.

The office is dark, auspicious, and very masculine.

Rachel enters hesitantly through the open door.

She watches Zelda for a long time. Zelda remains oblivious.

Finally Rachel inches forward, with surprising silence. She stands in front of the desk like an errant pupil.

Zelda looks up and freezes.

ZELDA. Oh my god.
RACHEL. Hi, I'm Rachel.
ZELDA. I'm Zelda. It's a pleasure to meet you. *(Rachel offers her hand. Zelda accepts it. Holds it a moment too long.)* Oh, I'm sorry.
RACHEL. That's okay.
ZELDA. Won't you sit?
RACHEL. Thank you. *(Rachel sits. Silence.)*
ZELDA. When did you arrive?
RACHEL. Just now.
ZELDA. Did you take the bus? Or the train?
RACHEL. My boyfriend drove me.

ZELDA. Oh, is he outside?

RACHEL. No, he went into town. He's going to pick me up in a bit.

ZELDA. Oh. Wonderful. *(Silence.)*

RACHEL. So thanks for seeing me. I hope I didn't freak you out or anything.

ZELDA. Freak me out?

RACHEL. By just calling, out of the blue.

ZELDA. You didn't freak me out. I've been waiting for that call for quite some time now.

RACHEL. I wasn't ready until recently.

ZELDA. Please, don't explain, that will only make things worse.

RACHEL. Make things worse?

ZELDA. For me, I mean, not for you. *(Beat.)*

RACHEL. *(Confused.)* I'm sorry, have I offended you?

ZELDA. What?

RACHEL. Do you want me to leave?

ZELDA. What? Are you insane? Please sit. *(Rachel doesn't move.)* Or, if you prefer, I'll stand. *(Zelda stands up. Rachel doesn't know what to make of this. Maybe she laughs. Maybe she just sits in a chair across from Zelda. Zelda sits too.)* There. Isn't this nice? So. How should we begin?

RACHEL. Begin?

ZELDA. How would you like to proceed?

RACHEL. I … I don't know.

ZELDA. I would assume you've given it some thought.

RACHEL. Of course, I've —

ZELDA. Do you have questions you'd like to ask me?

RACHEL. I have a million, but —

ZELDA. The way I see it, your areas of curiosity must be divisible into the historical, the biological, and the psychological.

RACHEL. Would it … would it be okay if we just sat here for a second?

ZELDA. Of course. *(They sit in silence. Staring at each other.)*

RACHEL. I like your office.

ZELDA. Thank you.

RACHEL. It feels very … masculine.

ZELDA. You mean it feels significant.

RACHEL. No, I don't. *(More silence.)*

ZELDA. So, did you take the train or the bus?

RACHEL. No, my boyfriend / drove me.

ZELDA. *(Overlapping.)* Your boyfriend drove you. That's right. I must have had a small stroke. That was a joke, though at my age I really shouldn't kid. Oh dear, you look frightened. Forget I said anything. You are very beautiful.

RACHEL. I know.

ZELDA. Oh.

RACHEL. I'm sorry.

ZELDA. No, that's — it's good that you know.

RACHEL. I'm sorry, I'm terrible at compliments.

ZELDA. I understand, so am I.

RACHEL. Plus, I'm so fucking nervous.

ZELDA. *(Quietly.)* So am I. Would you like a drink?

RACHEL. It's ten A.M.

ZELDA. Yes, I suppose that is a little early.

RACHEL. What have you got?

ZELDA. Champagne. Seems appropriate.

RACHEL. Okay. *(Zelda opens a cabinet to reveal a little refrigerator and full bar. She pulls out a champagne bottle.)*

ZELDA. My colleagues gave this to me the day I won a big honor in my field called the Dobzhansky Prize. I've been saving it for just the right occasion. *(Zelda pops the cork and pulls out two paper cups. She fills both a little too high and hands one to Rachel.)* L'Chaim.

RACHEL. What are we toasting to?

ZELDA. To life. *(They drink. Rachel looks around the office.)* I'm sorry it's such a mess. We're hosting a big conference here this weekend for NOORB — the National Organization of Research Biologists — it's like the Olympics of Biology — and we've been frantic, trying to prepare for it. *(Rachel just nods.)* You said you're a scientist too? On the phone?

RACHEL. Yes, I am. I'm a grad student at NYU.

ZELDA. Fantastic. Chemistry? Physics?

RACHEL. Biology, actually.

ZELDA. Biology. You're kidding. What are the odds? Molecular, I assume? That's the hot specialty these days. Inner space, as it were. Of which I am blissfully ignorant —

RACHEL. Evolutionary.

ZELDA. Evolutionary biology?

RACHEL. Yes.

ZELDA. As in, my field?

RACHEL. I know, right? *(Beat. Zelda stares at Rachel.)* So I, of course, know all about the NOORB conference this weekend.

ZELDA. You're a graduate student in evolutionary biology at NYU.

RACHEL. I am.

ZELDA. That is extraordinary. *(Uncomfortable silence. Rachel looks around the room.)*

RACHEL. Who said that?

ZELDA. Sorry?

RACHEL. That quote on your wall.

ZELDA. Ah. *(Zelda goes to her wall and pulls off a little wooden plaque. Reading.)* "My candle burns at both ends; // It will not last the night; // But ah, my foes, and oh, my friends — // It gives a lovely light!"

RACHEL. It sounds familiar. Is it Byron?

ZELDA. No.

RACHEL. Tennyson.

ZELDA. Vincent.

RACHEL. Who?

ZELDA. Edna St. Vincent Millay.

RACHEL. A woman wrote that?

ZELDA. You sound surprised.

RACHEL. It just sounds so … ballsy.

ZELDA. She was, by all accounts. Vincent Millay.

RACHEL. Who is M?

ZELDA. Sorry?

RACHEL. "With love and admiration — "

ZELDA. Oh yes, M. Um, that would be Michael.

RACHEL. Who's Michael?

ZELDA. My … boyfriend.

RACHEL. You have a boyfriend?

ZELDA. It's a little ridiculous, I know, at my age.

RACHEL. What does he do?

ZELDA. He's an oncologist.

RACHEL. He sounds smart.

ZELDA. He is.

RACHEL. So we both have smart boyfriends. There. That's something in common. *(Zelda smiles. They both relax. A bit.)*

ZELDA. Your boyfriend's name is?

RACHEL. Dean.

ZELDA. Is he very handsome?

RACHEL. I think so.

ZELDA. That's good. With a name like Dean it would be a shame if he weren't. *(The office phone rings.)*

RACHEL. Do you want to get that?

ZELDA. No, that's alright I — I'll just let them — in fact — *(Zelda picks up the ringing phone and replaces it on the receiver, effectively hanging up on the caller.)*

RACHEL. What if that was important?

ZELDA. Nobody calls this landline but pesky students. If it were important, they would know to call my — *(Zelda's cell phone starts to ring on the desk.)* Cell. *(Zelda checks the caller ID.)* I'm terribly sorry, would you mind if I just —

RACHEL. Of course. *(Zelda answers the call.)*

ZELDA. Hello? Hello, darling. It's not a great time, I'm with … oh, I see, no that's alright, just tell me quickly … I see … yes, of course, Vienna it is then … I'm looking forward to it, I really am … yes, I'll call you later to discuss all the logistics … alright, you too. *(Zelda hangs up.)* Speak of the devil.

RACHEL. Was that Michael?

ZELDA. Yes.

RACHEL. He's taking you to Vienna? *(Beat.)*

ZELDA. He is indeed.

RACHEL. When?

ZELDA. After NOORB.

RACHEL. That's so nice.

ZELDA. He's a nice man. *(For a moment Zelda is distracted. Lost. Rachel watches her, carefully.)* I'm sorry, I — this is really an extraordinary day. What were we just discussing? Before I — was it your research?

RACHEL. My research? No.

ZELDA. Well, perhaps it should be.

RACHEL. You want to hear about my research?

ZELDA. A good place to begin. A rather neutral topic, isn't it?

RACHEL. Not to me. *(Zelda stops. Puts her hand on her heart. Looks at Rachel.)* Are you alright?

ZELDA. I'm fine … just give me a moment. I am so glad you said that. I feel the same way.

RACHEL. I applied to the NOORB conference.

ZELDA. You did?

RACHEL. I didn't get in.

ZELDA. Which one was your abstract?

RACHEL. Which one?

ZELDA. I read some of the submissions —

RACHEL. Why?

ZELDA. I'm on the board. *(Beat.)*

RACHEL. I didn't know that.

ZELDA. You should have. You should be familiar with whomsoever is on the board of all the conferences you apply to. That's just good sense. *(Beat. Rachel is offended.)*

RACHEL. Uh, it was about human menstruation.

ZELDA. That was your abstract?

RACHEL. You read it?

ZELDA. Not personally, no, but I certainly heard of it. It was — well, it was rather famous actually, among the post-docs —

RACHEL. Famous in a bad way?

ZELDA. What? No, no. It sounds like it shook people up.

RACHEL. Why wasn't it selected then?

ZELDA. I'm sorry?

RACHEL. If everyone was talking about it, why didn't you give it a slot in the conference? *(Beat.)*

ZELDA. An abstract needs two champions on the selection committee to even be reviewed by the board.

RACHEL. And mine didn't have that?

ZELDA. No, if I remember correctly, it only had one. *(Beat.)*

RACHEL. Who?

ZELDA. Uh. A former student of mine. A woman named Bethany Gillette.

RACHEL. Never heard of her. *(Beat.)*

ZELDA. You're upset.

RACHEL. I'm not.

ZELDA. You are and that's good. It's good that you're upset.

RACHEL. I just think your selection process kinda sounds like bullshit.

ZELDA. You're quite right. *(Tense silence.)* Yes, well, perhaps it was naïve of me to think that science could be our neutral topic. But wait! We weren't talking about research at all. We were talking about men. Let's return to that. They're much less incendiary. *(Rachel smiles. They both relax. A bit.)* Tell me about yours.

RACHEL. Dean?

ZELDA. How long have you been seeing each other?

RACHEL. Three years.

ZELDA. And what does Dean do?

RACHEL. He's a scientist.

ZELDA. Oh dear.

RACHEL. He's not like the rest of them.

ZELDA. Uh-huh.

RACHEL. No, really. You'd never know he was a scientist.

ZELDA. I'd know.

RACHEL. We're in the same program. At NYU.

ZELDA. So he's your age?

RACHEL. A year younger, actually.

ZELDA. Good. That's very good. *(Again, Zelda seems lost. For a moment. In another world. Pause.)* Are you planning to marry him?

RACHEL. No.

ZELDA. Why not?

RACHEL. Neither of us believe in the institution.

ZELDA. What's to believe?

RACHEL. Dean's parents divorced before he was born. Then they both married again and divorced again, so he doesn't think he has the gene for it.

ZELDA. And your parents?

RACHEL. They're dead.

ZELDA. You're kidding.

RACHEL. I wouldn't kid about something like that.

ZELDA. No, forgive me. I'm sorry, I just — I didn't know.

RACHEL. How would you?

ZELDA. When did they die?

RACHEL. Five years ago. I was in college.

ZELDA. Was there an accident or — ?

RACHEL. No. They were just old. He died of lung cancer. And then, she followed him, like a year later. She just kind of … lost her will to live.

ZELDA. I'm so sorry, Rachel. *(Rachel shrugs.)*

RACHEL. You never married, did you?

ZELDA. Ah, no, never.

RACHEL. Yeah, what's the point? It's so much more romantic to wake up every morning and know you're both there by *choice*. Not because you're bound together by law. *(Zelda studies Rachel carefully.)*

ZELDA. So he's your guy, then? This Dean?

RACHEL. Absolutely. He's my guy.

ZELDA. You should marry him. Make it official.

RACHEL. I just told you — I don't see the point of the institution.

ZELDA. I'll tell you the point. Tax cuts. And health benefits. Which may not seem significant to you now, but trust me, later on, especially once children enter into the picture —

RACHEL. Excuse me?

ZELDA. If you're certain — if you're absolutely certain that Dean is the only man you will ever want to be with — and sleep with — for the rest of your life, then do yourself a favor and get hitched. It will save you a fortune. *(Beat. Rachel stares at Zelda.)* It's just my opinion.

RACHEL. Which I didn't ask you for.

ZELDA. *(Surprised.)* I'm afraid I offended you.

RACHEL. You didn't.

ZELDA. You look angry.

RACHEL. You don't know me. Maybe this is my happy face. Why would I want *your* opinion? I don't even know why I'm telling you this. It really isn't any of your business.

ZELDA. Rachel —

RACHEL. Please, don't — don't call me that.

ZELDA. It's your name.

RACHEL. Yes, but it suddenly sounds … bizarre coming from you.

ZELDA. Bizarre, how?

RACHEL. Creepy, alright? It sounds creepy.

ZELDA. What should I call you?

RACHEL. Just don't … don't call me. This was a mistake. I have to go.

ZELDA. Where are you going?

RACHEL. I have to go call my lab. When I left New York this morning, I put one of my undergrads in charge of changing the saline solutions and I think he was high, so —

ZELDA. My dear girl —

RACHEL. I am *not* your girl.

ZELDA. Ms. Hardeman. How's that? *(Pause.)*

RACHEL. That's fine.

ZELDA. Suitably formal?

RACHEL. Yes.

ZELDA. Please sit down.

RACHEL. No.

ZELDA. Jesus. This is quite difficult.

RACHEL. Did you expect it to be easy?

ZELDA. Well, I think I'm trying a bit harder than you are.

RACHEL. Which is appropriate, isn't it? *(Beat.)*

ZELDA. I didn't mean to offend you. I am simply amazed by the options you seem to have before you. Marry him, don't marry him. You're a scientist. He's a scientist. You have the kids. He has the kids. It really is a tree of possibilities, isn't it? *(Rachel is still standing. She looks towards the door.)* I thought maybe you'd like to see some pictures.

RACHEL. Pictures?

ZELDA. You know, of other people, family members? Me, when I was younger?

RACHEL. No, thank you. This has been strange enough. I don't need to spend the rest of the morning gazing upon Zelda Mildred Kahn, age ten. *(Rachel holds out her hand. Zelda rises slowly, takes it.)*

ZELDA. *(Carefully.)* I hate my middle name.

RACHEL. Yeah, it's pretty bad.

ZELDA. I try never to reveal it. You must have done some sleuthing. *(Rachel gathers her bag, puts on her coat —)*

RACHEL. Not really. It's in your bio.

ZELDA. Which bio did you read?

RACHEL. The one on the conference website.

ZELDA. Posted under "Board Members"? *(Rachel freezes.)*

RACHEL. Shit.

ZELDA. I thought you didn't know that I was on the conference board.

RACHEL. Yes. I just remembered that too. *(Silence.)* I lied.

ZELDA. I gathered.

RACHEL. I do that sometimes.

ZELDA. Good to know.

RACHEL. Should I leave?

ZELDA. Would you like to?

RACHEL. I feel like I should.

ZELDA. I'd rather you stayed. *(Beat. Rachel sits down again.)* You're really something of a terror, aren't you?

RACHEL. Charles says I'm difficult.

ZELDA. Who's Charles?

RACHEL. Sorry. Charles Byrne. My advisor at NYU. Do you know him?

ZELDA. I've heard of him. How is he?

RACHEL. Oh, he's fantastic.

ZELDA. He sounds a bit patronizing.

RACHEL. Not at all.

ZELDA. He called you difficult.

RACHEL. You called me a terror.

ZELDA. But the word "terror" suggests a certain ferocity, someone to be contended with. *(Rachel shrugs.)* I myself acquired a reputation for being difficult in my youth. Though, back then I think the clinical term was "bitch."

RACHEL. If you were a man, you would have been celebrated for it.

ZELDA. But I'm not a man. Neither are you. I know it seems romantic in your youth to behave badly —

RACHEL. Who said I behave badly?

ZELDA. Charles said "difficult" —

RACHEL. Because I refuse to sleep with him. That's what he means. Difficult to fuck. *(Beat.)*

ZELDA. Well. You certainly seem to have it all figured out. *(Uncomfortable silence.)* Is there anything you want to ask me, Rachel? Anything at all? *(Rachel thinks.)*

RACHEL. What's it like to win the Dobzhansky Prize? *(Zelda is taken aback.)*

ZELDA. Uh, it's a thrill, of course.

RACHEL. You got it for the Grandmother Hypothesis.

ZELDA. I did, yes.

RACHEL. How old were you?

ZELDA. Young. Your age.

RACHEL. You were twenty-eight?

ZELDA. Twenty-nine.

RACHEL. Fuck.

ZELDA. Excuse me?

RACHEL. I'm so behind.

ZELDA. It's not a race. *(Beat. Rachel stares at the award.)* Why don't you tell me about your research?

RACHEL. You don't want to hear about my research.

ZELDA. Why not?

RACHEL. Because it kinda contradicts your research.

ZELDA. *(Amused.)* Do you think I'm scared?

RACHEL. Maybe.

ZELDA. My dear. I have thirty years of groundbreaking data behind me, dozens of publications, grants, and a handful of global awards that are very difficult to come by. You have, by all accounts, an interesting idea. Believe me, I want to hear it.

RACHEL. It's a very powerful idea.

ZELDA. Aren't they all.

RACHEL. It's going to change everything.

ZELDA. And by "change everything" you mean it's going to add another minor wrinkle into the incredibly cavernous foreheads of the couple dozen research biologists that actually bother to read scientific journals and can summon enough energy to care about a hypothesis that isn't their own.

RACHEL. No, I mean it's going to change everything. The way that women think about their bodies. The way that men think about women's bodies. The way that people have sex.

ZELDA. It's going to change the way people have sex.

RACHEL. Yes.

ZELDA. Well. Don't make me beg. *(Rachel looks at Zelda, suspiciously.)* I'm past the age where I have any interest in intellectual supremacy. These days, I'm simply looking for the truth. You might have it. *(Silence.)*

RACHEL. You know Ernst Mayr, the evolutionary biologist?

ZELDA. *(Smiling.)* I do.

RACHEL. Well, he said that in biology, every issue is understandable from two perspectives — the how and the why. The mechanism and the function. The immediate explanation and the eternal one. In the case of female menstruation, we know the how. We know an egg drops down from one of the ovaries, hangs out in the uterus, waiting for a sperm, and if none comes, the uterine lining sheds and it, along with the egg, gets flushed through the vagina in a monthly bloodbath. We know how it happens. But we don't know why. *(Beat. Rachel looks at Zelda. Zelda doesn't say anything.)* And we've never cared. Because for hundreds of years professional scientists have been exclusively male and they don't menstruate so they don't care. But every aspect of our physiology has evolved evolutionarily for a reason. And the reason that we menstruate has never been obvious to me. It doesn't make sense. It's so calorically expensive to shed an endometrial layer every freaking month. And for our prehistoric predecessors, who spent their whole lives malnourished, every calorie counted. Do you want to respond?

ZELDA. *(Confused.)* You haven't said anything yet.

RACHEL. Menstruation also limits the window of opportunity

for conception, which is the holy grail of evolution. So the benefit of menstruation has to somehow outweigh this tremendous cost. *(Again, Rachel stops. Again, nothing from Zelda.)* Do you disagree?

ZELDA. With what?

RACHEL. With my theory.

ZELDA. You haven't yet stated a theory.

RACHEL. Menstruation is a defense.

ZELDA. Against what?

RACHEL. The toxicity of sperm. *(Silence.)*

ZELDA. *(Impressed.)* My God, that's ballsy.

RACHEL. Think about it. Sperm are riddled with foreign matter, just by virtue of being the products of another person's body, not to mention all the microbes — bacteria, viruses, and parasites that men are carrying around on the tips of their rods and women have buried in their bush. You put a sperm under a microscope, do you know how much other shit you find hanging on? The little pimp has a pathogenic entourage. And they all get a free ride up into the poor defenseless uterus. It's like some pristine, glacial lake — away from everything and then in come the sperm and bam! Oil spill. So what do we do? We clean ourselves out. Every month, we flush. Get rid of the old, infected endometrial tissue. Grow something new. Say something.

ZELDA. That's quite a theory.

RACHEL. Why is there a flow of blood? You can slough dead tissue without bleeding. Our skin cells flake all the time. But to change the uterus, we have to bleed. Why?

ZELDA. To loosen the dead cells of the uterine layer.

RACHEL. If it was purely mechanical, our bodies could use water. But what does blood carry?

ZELDA. Immune cells.

RACHEL. Exactly. T cells, B cells. Macrophages that act like internal Windex and clean the shop. But why get rid of all that tissue? Why not just reabsorb it like we do with the lining of our stomachs? Because it's not good to reabsorb *infected* tissue. And now, here's the kicker. Why, when compared to other female mammals, is the human menstrual flow so much heavier?

ZELDA. Because we're bigger.

RACHEL. We're not bigger than gorillas.

ZELDA. Because we have more pathogens in our uteri.

RACHEL. And why would we have more pathogens?

ZELDA. Because we have more sex.

RACHEL. Exactly. Right. We fuck all the time — not just in heat. Not just to reproduce. We build up more pathogens. We bleed for a long period of time.

ZELDA. So, by this theory, sexually active women have heavier periods?

RACHEL. Probably, but the differential would be too negligible to quantify. The real test, I believe, lies in comparing the menstrual output of one species of primate to another and then evaluating the results in comparison to the sexual proclivity of the respective species.

ZELDA. What'd you find?

RACHEL. The data's inconclusive. Menstruation in nonhuman animals hasn't ever been studied systematically.

ZELDA. Have you conducted any of your own experiments?

RACHEL. No. I don't have access to monkeys.

ZELDA. The girl who read your abstract, Bethany? She's a former student of mine. She's down at the Yerkes Primate Center at Emory studying the childbearing practices of chimps. And bonobos, I think. The two of you must meet.

RACHEL. That would be great.

ZELDA. Do you know if the concentration of pathogens is most intense in a woman's uterus right before menstruation?

RACHEL. I assume it is.

ZELDA. But do you have the data?

RACHEL. They've proven menses is preceded and accompanied by a massive infiltration of pathogen-fighting immune cells into the endometrium in studies by Jones from 1930, Nugent from 1935, Gardley from 1950, Kaufold from 1980 —

ZELDA. That's not what I asked.

RACHEL. Do I have the data that proves that pathogen concentration is higher right before menstruation? Of course not. That's an incredibly invasive experiment that's never been done. It would involve sticking a probe into the uteri of hundreds of sexually active women, multiple times a month. Who's going to authorize that?

ZELDA. Also, you must have considered the fact that most prehistoric women spent their entire adult lives continually pregnant — *(Rachel is looking at Zelda, strangely.)* What's wrong?

RACHEL. It sounds like you've thought all of this through before.

ZELDA. I have, of course.

RACHEL. And yet, you've never published anything about it.

ZELDA. About why women menstruate? I've never had anything

worth publishing. In all my years of considering the physiology of the female reproductive system, I've never stumbled upon such a remarkable hypothesis. *(Pause.)*

RACHEL. Then you think I'm on to something.

ZELDA. Frankly, I think it's a bit revolutionary.

RACHEL. I thought it was a good idea. I mean — I was hoping — it came to me in a dream. I *knew* it was a good idea. *(Rachel starts to cry.)*

ZELDA. Is something wrong?

RACHEL. No. *(Rachel puts her head down on the table. Zelda reaches out a hand. It hovers above Rachel's hair for a moment, then Zelda pulls it back.)* I just get a little emotional sometimes when I talk about my hypothesis. Charles says if I ever win the Dobzhansky Prize, he's going to give me a Xanax before the ceremony so I don't embarrass myself. *(Rachel wipes her eyes.)* Do you have a tissue? *(Zelda takes out a box of tissues and passes it to Rachel. Rachel blows her nose.)*

ZELDA. I feel like this is going badly.

RACHEL. Let's be honest. Maybe there was no way it could have gone well.

ZELDA. I really like your hypothesis.

RACHEL. Thank you.

ZELDA. This little theory might very well make you famous, Rachel.

RACHEL. Not if it never gets published. *(Pause.)*

ZELDA. There's an open slot, actually.

RACHEL. What?

ZELDA. At NOORB. I just heard this morning. One of our presenters dropped out, so there's a spot available in the morning of the second day.

RACHEL. What are you saying?

ZELDA. I'm asking, if you'd like to —

RACHEL. You can't do that.

ZELDA. Do what?

RACHEL. You can't just offer me a presentation.

ZELDA. Why not?

RACHEL. Doesn't the whole board have to approve me?

ZELDA. Well technically, yes, but I don't think that will be a problem. I'll vouch for you.

RACHEL. *(Confused.)* As your daughter? *(Beat.)*

ZELDA. No. As a new member of the scientific community to whom I give my endorsement. It's a somewhat radical theory and it might be helpful to have the approval of somebody a bit older before you — well, throw yourself to the wolves, really. I'd want to read the whole abstract. Unless, of course, you feel it isn't ready —

RACHEL. *(Quickly.)* It's ready. That would be — I would be — I just need to run it by Dean, but I think we would both be thrilled.

ZELDA. Who's Dean?

RACHEL. My boyfriend.

ZELDA. Yes, of course — and you want to check with him because — no, nevermind. That's none of my business.

RACHEL. We were going to do it together.

ZELDA. Do what together?

RACHEL. Present my abstract. At NOORB. *(Beat.)*

ZELDA. You do realize it's highly unorthodox for anyone who didn't author the abstract to present it before a national conference of this magnitude.

RACHEL. What's the big deal?

ZELDA. The big deal is people will think Dean created your hypothesis. *(Beat.)* Which isn't true. *(Beat.)* Is it?

RACHEL. We bounce all our ideas off of each other.

ZELDA. Who came up with the theory of menstruation as a defense against the toxicity of sperm? *(Rachel doesn't answer.)* I thought it came to you in a dream.

RACHEL. Are you saying you won't introduce us both?

ZELDA. If Dean gets up on that podium with you, people are going to think of you two as one scientific mind.

RACHEL. That's okay with me.

ZELDA. It shouldn't be.

RACHEL. I get really anxious when I speak in public.

ZELDA. So take a beta blocker.

RACHEL. I'll present something solo the next year.

ZELDA. What makes you think you'll get in next year?

RACHEL. Then the year after.

ZELDA. Rachel, this theory is a revelation. Many scientists slave away their entire lives and never come close to anything like it.

RACHEL. And I dreamed it up at twenty-eight. So there'll be others.

ZELDA. *(To herself.)* Jesus.

RACHEL. Why does it matter so much to you? You like the theory, right? You said you liked the theory. Why does it matter who stands behind the podium? *(Zelda just stares at Rachel.)* I'm not worried about my career. I've already co-authored three articles with Charles for *Science* magazine. I won the Ruth L. Kirschstein award from the NIH. I also won the National Science Foundation's postdoctoral fellowship for next year. I'm going to be fine.

ZELDA. And how's Dean doing? In the program?

RACHEL. He just co-created a groundbreaking new theory on the evolutionary imperative of hominid menses.

ZELDA. And otherwise? He's in danger of being cut, isn't he? *(Rachel looks at Zelda.)*

RACHEL. Can I smoke in here?

ZELDA. *(Surprised.)* You smoke?

RACHEL. Yes, sorry. It's a disgusting habit. I hate myself. Can I crack a window?

ZELDA. Be my guest. *(Rachel gets up, goes to a gothic window, and opens it. She takes out a pack of cigarettes, lights one, and inhales. Zelda watches the whole event, fascinated.)* You do realize that's a known carcinogen, right?

RACHEL. I've heard. *(Zelda crosses to the window seat to join Rachel. Rachel offers her a cigarette.)*

ZELDA. I quit. *(Rachel rolls her eyes. Takes another drag. And relaxes. A little bit.)*

RACHEL. Dean has one of the best minds at the lab. But nobody knows that because Dean doesn't speak up. He's shy. And he hasn't hit upon that one thing yet that will make his career —

ZELDA. And time is running out.

RACHEL. People expect it to take women longer. If I don't hit anything for another three or five or ten years, it's fine. In fact, if I hit it any earlier, they're liable to get suspicious. Who was helping me? Whose idea is this, really?

ZELDA. That's not as true as you'd like it to be. A good idea is a good idea. You have a good idea. People will see that, regardless of your gender, regardless of your age.

RACHEL. I couldn't have done it without Dean. *(Zelda sighs.)* He teased it out with me. Came at it from another angle. He made it watertight.

ZELDA. It's not watertight. Nothing is.

RACHEL. Will you introduce us both? Or just me? *(Zelda doesn't say anything.)* He works so hard. He deserves a little recognition in his field. I know you think I'm committing some sort of heinous crime, but I know what I'm doing. I want a family. I want children.

I want a full life. I don't want to end up alone with my research in thirty years.

ZELDA. Like your mother. *(Beat.)*

RACHEL. That's not what I'm saying. I didn't say that. I wasn't talking about you.

ZELDA. You seem very much in love.

RACHEL. I am.

ZELDA. I never married.

RACHEL. I know.

ZELDA. Why do you think I never married?

RACHEL. Because you cherished your independence.

ZELDA. Yes. And because nobody ever asked. When I was young, I made it clear that I didn't need anybody in my life. I took lovers, I left lovers. Old, young, men and women — I saw myself as an explorer. A sexual Magellan. I was not particularly good at monogamy, but in those days, nobody was. And I was lucky enough, as a young woman, to make an important discovery, which led to eventual tenure and financial security. So I didn't need to marry anyone to take care of me.

RACHEL. You're preaching to the choir. I'm not getting married.

ZELDA. And your Dean agrees?

RACHEL. Oh yes. He never wants to get married.

ZELDA. This equation doesn't add up. You don't want to marry him, but you're happy to wed him to your discovery. So you will be united, at least in the professional sense.

RACHEL. You're reading too far into this.

ZELDA. There's nothing wrong with wanting to marry the man you love.

RACHEL. I don't want to marry him!

ZELDA. You don't want to marry him or he doesn't want to marry you? *(Silence.)*

RACHEL. *(Stunned.)* You don't even know me.

ZELDA. Why doesn't Dean want to get married? Have you ever asked him?

RACHEL. He wants to build up a career first. Get published. Win a fellowship or two. He wants to be able to support me. And I respect that. I'm willing to wait.

ZELDA. Or you can just hand him the discovery right now. Speed the whole thing up.

RACHEL. That's not what I'm doing.

ZELDA. Are you sure?

RACHEL. First of all, it's just a theory. A *theory*. And second of all …
(Rachel stabs out her cigarette and stands up.) Fuck you. I should go.

ZELDA. I know this is uncomfortable.

RACHEL. *Uncomfortable?*

ZELDA. We all lie to ourselves to get through our lives. And then
every so often, somebody comes around and hands us a magic mirror.
It's a gift, really, though, at the time —

RACHEL. A magic mirror? Look, I've enjoyed meeting you. Forget
about presenting me, or Dean, at the conference. If I didn't get in, I
didn't get in. I don't need a favor from *you. (Rachel gathers her things.)*

ZELDA. Whose name was on the abstract?

RACHEL. What?

ZELDA. I'm just curious, since I never saw the application itself, did
it list both your names? *(Rachel starts for the door.)* You've come up
with a really good idea. It took rigor, it took study, it took courage
and it took genius. And it is *yours.* You created it. You gave *birth to
it.* Don't give it away because you're frightened of the implications. It
is yours. Keep the damn thing! *(Rachel stops at the door.)*

RACHEL. What about Dean?

ZELDA. Dean's big moment will come later. It sounds like he
needs a little longer to grow into himself. Into his own ideas. You're
wrong about the gender politics of science. Because he is a man, his
window of opportunity will be longer, not shorter.

RACHEL. He is all I have.

ZELDA. That's not entirely true, is it?

RACHEL. Yes. My parents are dead. The only person who gives
two shits about what happens to me is Dean. *(Pause.)*

ZELDA. What about your work?

RACHEL. My *work?*

ZELDA. You don't appreciate it — you can't appreciate it now.
You're too young. But trust me. It will save you. It will lift you and
it will hold you ten feet above whatever tempest descends. It is your
life vest, it is your therapy, it is the fountain of fucking youth. You
have been blessed. Believe me. *Believe me.* He'll understand. If he's
as good a man as you say he is, he'll be happy for you. That's the
key to surviving together in this field. You celebrate each other
through success, support each other through failure, but you do
not entangle alliances. And you do not compromise.

RACHEL. Does the Grandmother Hypothesis keep you warm at night?

ZELDA. As a matter of fact, it does. *(Rachel is still at the door. She doesn't know what to do.)*

RACHEL. You can't do that.

ZELDA. Do what?

RACHEL. Come back into my life after twenty-eight years and say, "I'm your mother. *Believe me.*"

ZELDA. What should I say? I've never done this either, Rachel. Tell me what you want to hear. *(Silence.)*

RACHEL. I read the Grandmother Hypothesis on the ride up. Your original dissertation.

ZELDA. My God. Why?

RACHEL. I've only studied it through secondary sources. It's such a polarizing theory. I wanted to know what you actually wrote.

ZELDA. What did you think?

RACHEL. Well … I didn't realize premature reproductive senescence wasn't identified until the fifties.

ZELDA. It's true.

RACHEL. So before then, nobody had noticed that human beings are the only primates to go through menopause? *(Zelda shrugs.)*

ZELDA. I'm sure they noticed.

RACHEL. But they hadn't bothered to study it.

ZELDA. George Williams came up with a theory around that time that said because it takes human children so long to grow up, their mothers had evolved to live longer.

RACHEL. *(Confused.)* That's not how evolution works.

ZELDA. I know. But back then, if anyone bothered to ask the question, that was the party line.

RACHEL. Until you went to study the Hadza. *(Zelda laughs.)*

ZELDA. No, until the mid-seventies, when the guys finally became interested in estrogen.

RACHEL. Because, given post-menopause, it seemed to prolong a woman's life.

ZELDA. Right. So, suddenly, everyone was curious — if estrogen is so good for women, why do they stop making it?

RACHEL. Which brought menopause as an evolutionary imperative under scrutiny?

ZELDA. Exactly. Because if estrogen is the life-force, then what were post-menopausal women still doing alive? Maybe it was just a lucky break. The consequence of modern medicine. Maybe they're all just lame ducks. *(Beat. Rachel thinks.)*

RACHEL. Have you ever read "The Nascence of Senescence"?

ZELDA. Henry Mortimer's paper? Of course. It's seminal.

RACHEL. The Grandmother Hypothesis basically repudiates it.

ZELDA. Well, it's also wrong. "The Nascence of Senescence" states that prehistoric woman died off when their eggs did. That is simply not true. I had the proof.

RACHEL. This proof … it was the Hadza?

ZELDA. That's right. They're primordial. Nomadic. They speak in clicks. They're as close as we come to a community living under Pleistocene conditions in modernity, and yet, they experience menopause. Those women routinely live into their seventies.

RACHEL. So menopause is natural.

ZELDA. I think so.

RACHEL. But the "why" still remains. What's the point?

ZELDA. The point is simply this: Prehistoric women were continually pregnant. But childbirth is exhausting and breastfeeding is so calorically expensive that a mother was barely able to eat enough to keep her infant alive. She had no time or energy to forage for her older children. For those children to reach maturity, they needed another guardian. A woman without responsibilities.

RACHEL. A grandmother.

ZELDA. A grandmother, correct. So the lucky women who lived longer in the Pleistocene epoch helped their grandchildren reach maturity. Thus, their gene pool thrived. And adapted towards longer life.

RACHEL. Which eventually allowed us to evolve beyond monkeys?

ZELDA. Precisely. Monkey mothers breastfeed their children for four or five years, but after that, they won't peel them a fucking banana. The simian child grows strong and stays stupid because his brain becomes concentrated on finding food. But the human child, who has a grandmother to peel his bananas, can stay weak and grow smart. His brain can continue to develop. He can think complex thoughts. So in a sense, when women started raising their children's children, they invented childhood, which in consequence, created humanity. *(Pause.)*

RACHEL. That's actually a fucking gorgeous theory.

ZELDA. Thank you.

RACHEL. And you tell it so well.

ZELDA. I've had thirty years to get comfortable talking about it. One day you'll feel the same way about your hypothesis. After you've defended it to thousands of people, it becomes like an old lover. Someone you fell for years ago, when you were young and stupid. *(Beat.)*

RACHEL. You did your post-grad work at Columbia, right?

ZELDA. That's right.

RACHEL. Who was your advisor? *(Beat.)*

ZELDA. Henry Mortimer.

RACHEL. And he allowed that thesis to go through? *(Zelda shrugs.)*

ZELDA. Max Gluckman called science "any discipline in which the fool of this generation can go beyond the point reached by the genius of last generation."

RACHEL. Aren't you and Mortimer in the same generation?

ZELDA. No! He's almost twenty years older. I have great respect for Henry Mortimer. In many ways, our relationship sounds a lot like the one you have with your advisor.

RACHEL. But you didn't stay at Columbia.

ZELDA. No. That's true. I didn't. *(Silence. Zelda doesn't offer anything more. Rachel checks her watch.)*

RACHEL. *(Genuinely.)* It was … wonderful to meet you. I really have to go now. Dean is waiting for me.

ZELDA. They are going to want to dismiss you too. They will look for any excuse. I have been fighting for thirty years, with everything I have, to get people to listen to the Grandmother Hypothesis. To take seriously the claim, by a woman, that Adam never lost a rib. That we are not biologically, from a purely scientific standpoint, secondary. We are smaller, yes. We are weaker, yes. Our brains contain less mass, true, true, true. And yet, *we live longer.* And that is not an accident. That is evolution. You have no idea the work it has taken just to be heard, never mind believed. And the sacrifices I've … But I got here. And now, when I talk, people listen.

RACHEL. Was it worth it? *(Beat.)*

ZELDA. I was too young to raise a child.

RACHEL. How old were you? *(Beat.)*

ZELDA. Twenty-eight.

RACHEL. Okay. I guess we're different that way. *(Rachel puts out her hand to shake once again. Zelda grasps it, fervently.)*

ZELDA. But nobody is asking you to give up a child. All I'm asking you to do is give yourself a chance. You're standing right where I was — *(Zelda holds up Rachel's hand.)* With a theory in your palm that will liberate women from the shame of menses. And you're about to hand it off to your lover to keep peace in your bed. *(Rachel yanks her hand back.)* And you're too young to know that it's one of those mistakes you will never recover from. *(Rachel crosses back to the door.)* Where are you going?

RACHEL. Home.

ZELDA. Back to New York?

RACHEL. I guess.

ZELDA. You're not going to stay through NOORB?

RACHEL. I wasn't invited.

ZELDA. I will get you that slot. If it's you up at that podium or Dean or both of you. It is a good idea. It deserves to receive the greatest possible attention. *(Beat. The women just look at each other.)*

RACHEL. Thank you.

ZELDA. You have three days to prepare.

RACHEL. I know.

ZELDA. Would you like to meet again? There are a few other things I'm unclear about.

RACHEL. Like what?

ZELDA. Well, for example, blood contains iron, which is one of the things bacteria needs to proliferate. So wouldn't all that menstrual blood promote uterine infection, rather than dissolve it?

RACHEL. It would unless our bodies had created some way to sequester the iron. Such as immune cells secreting lactoferrin in high density to bind to the iron and make it unusable to bacteria. And it just so happens, in a 1978 study, plasma levels of lactoferrin were found to be twice as high in the endometrium right before menses than during the mid-cycle. *(Rachel smiles at Zelda.)*

ZELDA. I have other questions.

RACHEL. Ask them at the Q and A. It will give me a way to quiet the thunderous applause. *(Rachel goes. Zelda sips her champagne. Lights down. A break.)*

Scene 2

A dive bar.

Rachel is waiting there, nervously. She keeps looking at her watch.

She stands up to leave.

Zelda walks in.

She spots Rachel, waves, and comes over to her table.

ZELDA. I'm so sorry I'm late.

RACHEL. It's okay.

ZELDA. It's not okay. I shouldn't have kept you waiting. I seem to be late to everything lately. I don't know where my mind is. We almost missed our flight back from Vienna because I — oh never mind, it's not important. Do they serve food here? I'm starving. *(Rachel just stares at her.)* You do eat, don't you dear? I've been meaning to ask you that. Do you eat? Because you look thin. And perhaps that's your natural body type. But it isn't my natural body type and it wasn't your father's, so I've been meaning to ask you, do you eat?

RACHEL. What's my father's body type? *(Beat. Zelda looks at Rachel.)*

ZELDA. Later. Later we will discuss your father. And his body type. And his sexual proclivities, if you're interested, which you may not be. But first, we must order food. Though, I gained seven pounds in three days in Vienna. Between the bread and the lard and cream sauce and all that pig product. I don't know how the Austrians stay so thin. Actually I do. They smoke like chimneys. *(Zelda looks around the dingy little space for a waiter.)* I used to be thin like that, when I smoked.

RACHEL. How much did you smoke?

ZELDA. About a pack a day.

RACHEL. *A pack a day?*

ZELDA. Yes and I regret every second of it. You must quit. *(Zelda can't find a waiter anywhere.)*

27

RACHEL. How did you quit?

ZELDA. I got pregnant with you. What are you drinking?

RACHEL. Bourbon.

ZELDA. Wow. You really can drink. You didn't get that from me. But perhaps I'll have some wine. They do serve wine here, don't they?

RACHEL. It's probably from a box.

ZELDA. From a box? That's outrageous. Waiter! *(Zelda is just signaling into the ether. Rachel rolls her eyes.)*

RACHEL. You have to go up to the bar and order it.

ZELDA. Charming. *(Zelda starts to rise. Rachel shoots the rest of her bourbon down.)*

RACHEL. I'll get it. White or red?

ZELDA. *(Bewildered.)* White. *(Rachel gathers her empty glass and goes to the bar. Zelda tries to make herself at home. The place is much dirtier than she's used to. Rachel returns with two drinks. She sits.)* Thank you.

RACHEL. How was Vienna?

ZELDA. How was Vienna. Well, Vienna, from what I saw of it, was amazing. Like a little city out of time. And the Austrians … they're so … rational. They are observational empiricists, every one. Really, it was just heaven. If you and Dean ever have the opportunity to go, I'll give you the name of the little inn where I stayed. I had a room in the attic.

RACHEL. How's Michael? *(Beat.)*

ZELDA. He's good. Lovely man.

RACHEL. I thought he might propose to you there.

ZELDA. Propose? For heaven's sake.

RACHEL. Why else do people fly off to Vienna for a weekend?

ZELDA. He didn't propose.

RACHEL. I'm sorry.

ZELDA. Don't be. *(A beat. Zelda raises her glass.)*

RACHEL. What are we drinking to?

ZELDA. To you, my dear. And your achievement at the conference.

RACHEL. My achievement?

ZELDA. The speech was quite spectacular. Beautifully articulated. Gloriously original. And brave. Really, most of all, terrifically brave. The room around you just crackled. Did you feel that? *(Beat.)*

RACHEL. They hated me.

ZELDA. I don't think that's true.

RACHEL. Have you been reading the blogs?

ZELDA. The what?

RACHEL. The scientific blogs. On the internet?

ZELDA. No.

RACHEL. I've read at least a dozen blog posts in response to the NOORB conference.

ZELDA. If all these people are blogging, who is running their labs?

RACHEL. One blog talked about the "horror show" that was Rachel Hardeman's NOORB presentation. Another said if NOORB was so desperate for female presenters this year, they would have been better off asking a high school science teacher to discuss what her students had discovered in their petri dishes. Another said he couldn't pay attention to my talk because the name I had given my primate prototype reminded him of a porn star.

ZELDA. What was her name again?

RACHEL. Bloody Mary.

ZELDA. What kind of porn is he watching?

RACHEL. Does it *matter*?

ZELDA. That was a joke. Rachel, welcome to the game. You wanted to play with the big boys — this is how they play.

RACHEL. That's not true. I've been to these conferences before. I've seen the criticism lobbied against other hypotheses. This was worse. They were specifically vicious towards me.

ZELDA. You don't think you're being a little paranoid?

RACHEL. No.

ZELDA. Why would they be specifically vicious towards you?

RACHEL. Because I am a woman. *(Beat.)*

ZELDA. Rachel, don't.

RACHEL. They dismissed me. They never even engaged my argument. I walked up there, in my skirt and my heels. I said sperm and pathogen in one sentence. I said menstruation and defense in another and they all stopped listening. I saw them stop.

ZELDA. You *saw* them stop *listening*.

RACHEL. Yes, and then, they went after me *personally*. Not my theories, my right to have them. They had done their homework. At the cocktail hour afterwards, these two board members came up to me and they basically implied that if I had known my father, I might be less suspicious of sperm.

ZELDA. That doesn't make any sense.

RACHEL. I know! And do you know what they'd have to do find out I was adopted? They'd have to hire a private investigator!

ZELDA. I don't think anyone did that. Everyone's bio gets printed in the conference program.

RACHEL. My bio doesn't say that the people who raised me were not my direct genetic predecessors.

ZELDA. I might have brought it up to the board.

RACHEL. What?

ZELDA. Everyone was so impressed by your abstract and how young you are, they wondered if you came from a family of scientists. So I said no ... that I knew you a bit personally ... and that you were adopted —

RACHEL. You said you "knew me a bit personally"?

ZELDA. If you'll allow me to give you a piece of advice — do not turn the reaction to your hypothesis into an issue of sexism, not in your own mind, and certainly not in public. It will do nothing for you. You're worried about being discredited? That will discredit you.

RACHEL. I've already been discredited.

ZELDA. Stop it. No, you haven't. You presented a very progressive theory to the national organization at an annual conference and it received mixed responses. It is an honor to have presented at the conference at all, and if you don't do anything stupid, you have the rest of a lengthy career to recover.

RACHEL. To *recover*?

ZELDA. I mean, to review your hypothesis and make improvements.

RACHEL. I thought you loved my hypothesis.

ZELDA. I like it very much. I do.

RACHEL. You just said it needs improvements.

ZELDA. *(Frustrated.)* You are twenty-eight years old! You don't think you have anything left to learn? *(Silence.)* Were you able to hear — to really hear any of the questions the audience asked?

RACHEL. *(Incredulous.)* You think I should have changed Mary's name?

ZELDA. One pointed out that monthly menstruation is a modern phenomenon. Because our ancestors were constantly pregnant or amenorrheic, so they didn't need to expel their uterine lining. Which, when last we met, was something I suggested you really should consider —

RACHEL. I did consider it.

ZELDA. Why hadn't you prepared a defense?

RACHEL. I had.

ZELDA. Well ... why didn't you share it when he asked the question?

RACHEL. He didn't ask a question. He just made a statement and then, if you remember correctly, there was a cacophony of applause. Applause! But before I could tell them why it was the most overly simplistic, reductionist response to what I had proposed, some other fifty-year-old, balding asshole jumped up with another dogmatic "question," which I, again, wasn't given the opportunity to respond to. And then, of course, there was Bethany.

ZELDA. Ah yes, Bethany. Well, if we're considering things through your worldview, that was a stroke of very bad luck. If we're considering things through mine, and I sincerely hope we soon will be, it could also have been the opportunity for a really lively debate. Who knew Bethany would have such explicit evidence at her fingertips?

RACHEL. Well, you for one. You knew.

ZELDA. I knew?

RACHEL. She's one of your former students after all. Isn't she?

ZELDA. Bethany worked in my lab, fifteen years ago. *As an undergrad.*

RACHEL. Still, she was a reader for the conference. Clearly, you've been in touch. It's only natural to assume she's been keeping you abreast of her research, isn't it? *(Beat.)*

ZELDA. Yes, and Bethany's work concerns the childbearing practices of monkeys. Not the evolutionary necessity of human menstruation. I had no idea she'd completed a phylogenic analysis of the menses of primates. Why would she? It's completely tangential to her research. She said she did it because she was curious.

RACHEL. And see — that right there. That seems suspicious to me.

ZELDA. Why would I deliberately create a competition between you and Bethany?

RACHEL. Between your biological daughter and your adopted one? I don't know. Nature versus nurture?

ZELDA. What kind of person do you think I am?

RACHEL. I have no fucking idea what kind of a person you are. You gave me away when I was six days old. *(Silence.)*

ZELDA. I hadn't seen Bethany in fifteen years. I had no idea what specific experiments her current research entailed. But I was thrilled to find out she held the missing link. The experiment comparing the menstrual output of one species of primate to another. The experiment you thought had never been done.

RACHEL. You were *thrilled*?

ZELDA. Yes. For you. As a scientist. Thrilled that you would finally have the truth. The fact that Bethany's research found little connection between the sexual proclivity of a species and the heaviness of its menstrual flow, as you hypothesized — well, that is disappointing. But it's information you should be glad to have. If you are at all serious about this theory of yours. About evolutionary biology. About science in general. About yourself, for God's sake. If you're interested in pursuing this for any other reason than to get back at me. *(Beat.)*

RACHEL. Is that what you think I'm doing?

ZELDA. Why did you go into this discipline?

RACHEL. I was *interested* in it.

ZELDA. See, *that* I find suspicious. You were interested in pursuing a career in my *exact* field?

RACHEL. I didn't know it was your field. I didn't know who the hell you were.

ZELDA. So what was so "interesting" to you about evolutionary biology? *(Rachel stares at Zelda.)*

RACHEL. When normal people want to make sense of their idiosyncratic physiology, they just look at their mother or father. But my mother and father were complete genetic strangers. So I had to study the human fucking race. *(Beat.)*

ZELDA. That makes sense. That's just what I would have done.

RACHEL. I didn't find out who you were until I called the adoption agency two weeks ago. I thought it was a joke. I thought someone was playing a trick on me.

ZELDA. Well, I didn't know about Bethany. That's the God's honest truth. *(Silence.)*

RACHEL. I never expected it to come from a woman.

ZELDA. What?

RACHEL. The criticism. The most … injurious criticism. I expected it to come from a man. But not a woman. I thought we were all on the same team.

ZELDA. Yes, well, that was naïve of you.

RACHEL. Bethany basically accused me of misogyny. She said my hypothesis suggests a woman's sexual promiscuity is measurable by her volume of menstrual output.

ZELDA. I did try to warn you that that was one possible misinterpretation of your hypothesis.

RACHEL. But you knew, *you knew*, that wasn't my intention. And yet, you said nothing.

ZELDA. What could I have said?

RACHEL. Something. Anything. You said I was brilliant. You said you *believed* in me.

ZELDA. Rachel, I introduced you. I gave you my blessing.

RACHEL. Sure, and then as soon as they started to attack me, you disappeared. I looked around the room for you. When I was up there, under siege, I tried to find you. Anything from you. A gesture. A smile. Even eye contact —

ZELDA. Really? If I had winked at you in that moment, all your problems would have evaporated?

RACHEL. *(Desperately.)* Where did you go?

ZELDA. *(Beat.)* I wasn't feeling well. I went to the bathroom.

RACHEL. You went to the bathroom. While I was up there, being broiled alive.

ZELDA. I thought you were a grown-up. I didn't realize you needed me to hold your hand.

RACHEL. Was it an emergency?

ZELDA. I beg your pardon?

RACHEL. Did you really, *really* have to go?

ZELDA. That isn't your business. *(Beat.)*

RACHEL. When, exactly, did you go to the bathroom?

ZELDA. I'm not having this conversation.

RACHEL. Did you stay until the end of my presentation?

ZELDA. Of course.

RACHEL. So it was around the time they started to ask questions. *(Zelda stares at Rachel.)* I'm just wondering if you stayed in the room long enough to realize I was going down.

ZELDA. The only person who believes you "went down" at the conference is you! Everyone else witnessed the courageous, invigorating presentation of an exciting young talent, who *lost it*, at the first whisper of criticism.

RACHEL. So you stayed long enough to see me crack. And then you left because you didn't want to prolong your association with failure. I guess I really should have anticipated that. This is sort of your forte, isn't it? Abandoning your mistakes? *(Zelda slaps Rachel across the face. A beat. Rachel stands, slowly.)*

ZELDA. Sit down.

RACHEL. Go to hell. *(Rachel crosses to the door.)*

ZELDA. Where are you going?

RACHEL. What does it matter?

ZELDA. What will you do now?

RACHEL. Why do you care?

ZELDA. Will you continue to refine your hypothesis or shift your concentration to something else? *(Rachel doesn't answer.)* Rachel?

RACHEL. I don't know, okay? I have no fucking idea what to do now. I want to shift my concentration to bringing Bethany Gilette to her fucking knees. I've been playing the questions over and over again in my mind … and here's the thing, nobody offered up a counter-hypothesis. They poked holes in my theory, but nobody had another explanation for why women menstruate. Which means, I'm still probably right. I just need to prove Bethany and her butt-licking monkeys wrong. I'm not worried. She's probably falsifying the fuck out of that data. *(Beat.)*

ZELDA. It might be better if you didn't think of science as such a competitive sport —

RACHEL. Don't be ridiculous. Of course it is.

ZELDA. Bethany is a good scientist. You might not agree with all of her findings, but you can't just erase them. You have to be willing to hear criticism.

RACHEL. I can hear criticism.

ZELDA. Good, because there is something I wanted to tell you. When I was in Vienna, I had the opportunity to visit the Institute of Biological Sciences, where I spoke with their chief scientist who is an ex-lover of mine. She —

RACHEL. She?

ZELDA. Yes. I told her about your hypothesis. She found it fascinating but entirely misguided. According to Marie, menstruation is not as calorically expensive as *not* menstruating. As maintaining a uterine lining at conception-ready conditions *all the time*. With all the hormones, proteins, fats, sugars required to sustain a fetus — do you know how much oxygen that endometrium requires?

RACHEL. A lot.

ZELDA. A tremendous amount. So couldn't it be more cost effective to shed the layer each month? Grow another one the next month. Try again? And all that blood? That you claim cleanses. There's another explanation. Tiny spiral arteries weave together around the uterus each month to provide the placenta with blood if a pregnancy were to occur. When the endometrium dies and flushes out of the body, it takes the tips of these arteries with it.

RACHEL. That makes sense.

ZELDA. Yes, well, there's your counter-hypothesis.

RACHEL. How old is Marie?

ZELDA. What does that have to —

RACHEL. She's your age, isn't she?

ZELDA. Yes.

RACHEL. From the generation of martyrs.

ZELDA. The generation of what?

RACHEL. "According to Marie," we women bleed each month so that, when the time comes, our fetuses can drink our blood. How noble of us. How selfless. So much better than an anti-pathogen theory, with its erotic overtones and carnal implications. Of course, everyone would much prefer a theory in which women bleed to sustain their babies rather than to protect themselves from penises. Even if it's wrong. You fucking feminists. You're so hypocritical. You go on and on about female empowerment and all you did for us, but the truth is, you're ten times harder on us than anybody else. *(Beat.)*

ZELDA. Women keep having sex well into menopause. How then do they continue to protect themselves from sperm? If menstruation is a woman's natural defense against the toxicity of sperm, why should this system shut down so many years before a woman stops having sex? *(Rachel sighs.)*

RACHEL. It shouldn't.

ZELDA. Precisely. But that doesn't mean your theory is wrong. It's just not complete.

RACHEL. The reason we don't continue to menstruate after menopause is because we are not biologically intended to live past menopause. My theory isn't wrong. Yours is. *(Beat.)*

ZELDA. You mean it's inconvenient.

RACHEL. I mean the Grandmother Hypothesis is wrong. Don't take it personally. *(Silence. Zelda stares at Rachel.)*

ZELDA. Maybe you're right. Maybe the Grandmother Hypothesis needs revision.

RACHEL. What?

ZELDA. Theories are mortal. Just like the people who create them. I've been waiting a long time for someone to come along and kill mine off. What a relief. You're finally here. *(Beat. Rachel frowns.)*

RACHEL. What are you doing?

ZELDA. What do you mean?

RACHEL. Is this some sort of reverse psychology?

ZELDA. No.

RACHEL. Are you trying to get me to renounce my theory?

ZELDA. Why would you do that? You haven't even published. *(Beat.)*

RACHEL. You're frightened of me.

ZELDA. Come again?

RACHEL. Of course you are. How did I miss that? *(Zelda laughs.)*

ZELDA. You can't be serious.

RACHEL. You went all the way to Vienna to find someone who would refute me.

ZELDA. I was trying to help you.

RACHEL. Bullshit. You're terrified. That's why you got me the spot at the conference. You knew my theory wasn't ready —

ZELDA. I *knew*? More to the point, why didn't *you* know?

RACHEL. I've never done this before. I didn't know they go for blood. But you did. You just threw me up there. Knowing what would happen. You *wanted* it to happen. Because I scare the shit out of you. *(Silence. Zelda sips her wine. Takes a deep breath.)*

ZELDA. I was thinking, since you're still in town, maybe I could have you and Dean over to dinner. I would like to spend time with him. Get to know him.

RACHEL. We broke up.

ZELDA. What?

RACHEL. Dean and I broke up.

ZELDA. When?

RACHEL. After NOORB. Or maybe it was during. I don't know. He left a note.

ZELDA. He left a note? What did it say?

RACHEL. He said he could tell he was no longer a priority for me.

ZELDA. Oh, Rachel. You must be angry.

RACHEL. At whom?

ZELDA. At Dean!

RACHEL. Not really. I'm angry at myself. And a little bit at you. I'm angry at myself for listening to you. I should have just let him share that stupid presentation. *(Beat.)*

ZELDA. Who wrote the abstract?

RACHEL. That doesn't matter.

ZELDA. That's the only thing that matters.

RACHEL. No, the only thing that matters — the only thing that has ever mattered — is *Dean*. In the dream I was at a rally. Like some sort of communist rally, but it was all women. We were wearing red

36

armbands. They hoisted a red flag. And out of nowhere, a man dressed in black appeared. He raised a gun and he shot the flag. It made a black hole in the red fabric. And as the flag fluttered, slowly, the whole thing turned black. I woke up, spooked. I woke Dean up. I told him about it. And he said, *he said*, it's a dream about sex.

ZELDA. Rachel, I could have told you that was a dream about sex.

RACHEL. But you didn't. He did. And without him, I wouldn't have thought twice about that dream. We stayed up all night together. We teased out all the possibilities and in the morning we had come up with the theory. Together. But because I listened to you and your bullshit, I wouldn't even let him share the stage —

ZELDA. Who wrote the abstract?

RACHEL. It doesn't matter!

ZELDA. *Who wrote the abstract?*

RACHEL. You're not *listening* to me.

ZELDA. I'm sorry things didn't work out between you and Dean. But that is just further evidence of his tremendous immaturity. He doesn't have the ability, the decency, to be happy for you and your achievements —

RACHEL. What did I achieve? I was publicly humiliated and I lost the only person who ever believed in me.

ZELDA. You believe in you.

RACHEL. What?

ZELDA. What Dean thinks doesn't matter. What I think doesn't matter. The only person whose opinion needs to matter to you is yours. *(Silence.)*

RACHEL. Have you ever loved *anyone*? *(Beat.)*

ZELDA. Yes.

RACHEL. I mean, really loved them. Enough to give up everything for them?

ZELDA. No. Because that sort of love does not exist. It is a fantasy that cowardly young women tell themselves to avoid the reality that they voluntarily fucked up their lives.

RACHEL. That isn't true.

ZELDA. If your love affair with Dean was so extraordinary, how come it fell apart so easily? Have you asked yourself that?

RACHEL. Because love is fucking magic. And like magic, you have to believe in it. You make an agreement — both of you — it's unspoken, but it's there — to put the other person first. In every decision you make. Because you know, somewhere in the deepest

part of your soul, that is what will make your life worth living!
(Zelda looks at her, calmly.)

ZELDA. You want to know what love is? It's stress. It's just stress. Certain species with a vigorous stress response axis, whose adrenal glands release a high amount of cortisol, those are the species that fall in love often. Such as the prairie vole. Sex is an act of aggression. It triggers a stress response, which makes the woman being penetrated attach to the man on top of her. Basically, love is the Stockholm syndrome, gussied up. It may sound laughable, but it's biological. I don't like it, but I respect it. I have succumbed to it in the past, but I refuse to let something so *ordinary* define me. I am smarter than a prairie vole. I have a mind. And I intend to use it. I thought, perhaps, you intended to use yours as well. I see now that I was wrong. Go back to Dean. Grovel. Give him a blowjob. I'm sure you'll be fine.
(Beat. Rachel stares at her mother. A realization.)

RACHEL. You must be so lonely. You've spent your whole life alone, with your face in a microscope. *(Zelda sighs.)*

ZELDA. You could look at it that way. I think it's the most thrilling possible way to spend one's time. The chance that in every minute of every day you might stumble across even the smallest secret of the universe. And for a moment, this new truth will be known only to you. *(Silence.)*

RACHEL. Charles doesn't teach the Grandmother Hypothesis.

ZELDA. Who's Charles?

RACHEL. My advisor at NYU.

ZELDA. Why not?

RACHEL. Charles says you couldn't find mitochondria with the Hubble telescope. *(Beat.)*

ZELDA. Nobody could find mitochondria with a telescope.

RACHEL. It's a joke.

ZELDA. It isn't a very good one.

RACHEL. Charles says you belong to a group of women scientists who, in the seventies, thought with their vaginas.

ZELDA. My God.

RACHEL. Charles says you used some scientific voodoo to conjure a primitive matriarch from beneath the earth and give her back her powers. But she's been dead since mankind realized that sperm is the catalyst of creation. Everyone but you can clearly see she is nothing more than a rotting corpse with a crown on her head. *(Silence.)*

ZELDA. Well. That is depressing.

RACHEL. Do you know Charles?

ZELDA. Only by reputation.

RACHEL. He did his post-doc work at Columbia.

ZELDA. Did he.

RACHEL. He had Henry Mortimer as an advisor too.

ZELDA. Henry's a very famous scientist. He advised a lot of people.

RACHEL. So you never overlapped?

ZELDA. With Charles? I don't know. What years was he there?

RACHEL. I think he started in '80.

ZELDA. I was in Africa by then. So no, we never overlapped. *(Silence.)*

RACHEL. You left to go study the Hadza.

ZELDA. That's right.

RACHEL. Did you live with them?

ZELDA. For a while.

RACHEL. They walk a lot, don't they? Like, twenty miles a day?

ZELDA. They do, yes.

RACHEL. You could keep up with them?

ZELDA. I was in pretty good shape when I was young.

RACHEL. Even though you smoked a pack a day?

ZELDA. I had quit by then.

RACHEL. You said you quit when you got pregnant with me. But I wasn't born until 1983. Something about this equation doesn't add up, Zelda. *(Zelda sips her wine.)* Who's my father? *(No response.)* Is it Charles?

ZELDA. Charlie Byrne. God, no.

RACHEL. Who is it then?

ZELDA. Rachel, use your head.

RACHEL. My head says it's Charles.

ZELDA. Well, use somebody else's head then. *(Beat.)*

RACHEL. I think you were running away from someone at Columbia. *(Beat.)* Henry? *(Zelda just looks at her.)* Henry Mortimer? *(Zelda nods.)* Oh my God. Henry Mortimer is my fucking father?? *(Zelda looks around the bar, embarrassed.)*

ZELDA. Is it really that big a deal?

RACHEL. Are you kidding me? The Father of Hormone Replacement Therapy?

ZELDA. You do realize that all of his clinical studies were underwritten by the pharmaceutical companies, right?

RACHEL. So?

ZELDA. So, perhaps a more measured response to his historical significance —

RACHEL. *The Eternal Female* sold over a million copies. When has that *ever* happened to an evolutionary biologist?

ZELDA. By saying menopause was entirely avoidable! *(Rachel just looks at Zelda, blankly.)* Oh for God's sake, Rachel, he's been debunked.

RACHEL. I cannot believe Henry Mortimer is my father.

ZELDA. Doesn't it bother you that the very existence of HRT implies that a woman's body doesn't know what it's doing? That it needs to be supplemented with hormones it has naturally elected to stop producing? Just look at the word he chose to *name* it. Therapy. As if menopause was some sort of deficiency. It's all *marketing*. Our bodies are not sick. Estrogen is not a drug. Given in excess, it's been proven carcinogenic.

RACHEL. So what?

ZELDA. Doesn't it bother you?

RACHEL. Not really. Does it bother you?

ZELDA. Yes, it does.

RACHEL. Maybe because his hypothesis ultimately proved more popular than yours —

ZELDA. No. Because I have cancer. *(Silence.)*

RACHEL. What?

ZELDA. That's why I was in Vienna. To receive an experimental treatment.

RACHEL. You said you went to Vienna with some dude named Michael.

ZELDA. I did. He's my oncologist.

RACHEL. You said he was your boyfriend.

ZELDA. I lied. I do that sometimes. *(Beat.)*

RACHEL. You have cancer.

ZELDA. Yes.

RACHEL. What kind?

ZELDA. Breast.

RACHEL. What phase?

ZELDA. Three.

RACHEL. Has it spread to the lymph nodes?

ZELDA. Yes. Some.

RACHEL. That's bad.

ZELDA. I know. There's a new clinical trial happening in Vienna. It hasn't been approved by the FDA ... So ...

RACHEL. Is it working?

ZELDA. I don't know yet. *(Beat.)* I didn't mean to abandon you. It's just … the chemo makes me … I needed to use the bathroom.

RACHEL. I don't know what to say. I'm sorry.

ZELDA. Thank you. *(Silence.)*

RACHEL. Did you take estrogen?

ZELDA. Yes.

RACHEL. When?

ZELDA. After you were born.

RACHEL. But you were so young. *(Beat.)*

ZELDA. I had a hysterectomy.

RACHEL. Why?

ZELDA. There were … complications with my placenta during my delivery. I couldn't stop bleeding. They had to remove my uterus.

RACHEL. During your delivery with me.

ZELDA. Yes.

RACHEL. That's why you never had any other children.

ZELDA. Yes.

RACHEL. And now you have cancer. *(Beat. Rachel suddenly drops her forehead to the table with a bang.)*

ZELDA. *(Alarmed.)* It isn't your fault. *(Rachel sits up, but something's wrong. She's breathing heavily.)* Are you okay? *(Rachel shakes her head.)* What's the matter?

RACHEL. I can't breathe.

ZELDA. Why not? *(Rachel starts to hyperventilate.)*

RACHEL. I can't breathe.

ZELDA. Rachel. Rachel! Look at me. You're fine.

RACHEL. *(Hoarsely.)* My throat's closing up.

ZELDA. Then breathe through your nose.

RACHEL. *(Hoarsely.)* Can you call an ambulance?

ZELDA. No.

RACHEL. *(Hoarsely.)* I can't breathe.

ZELDA. If you can speak, you can breathe.

RACHEL. *(Gasping.)* It might take them a while to get here! *(Zelda stands, gets behind Rachel, and rubs her back.)*

ZELDA. Just concentrate on breathing. In through your nose. Out through your mouth. Ready? In … two … three. Out … two … three. In through your nose, out through your mouth. In … two … three. Out … two … three … *(Rachel breathes as Zelda keeps chanting instructions. She slowly starts to calm down. Finally, she stops hyperventilating.)* Better? *(Rachel nods.)*

RACHEL. That breathing thing works.

ZELDA. Lamaze.

RACHEL. What?

ZELDA. Never mind. That looked exhausting. Let's get you something to eat. Can you order anything here? *(Zelda signals the bartender offstage.)* Food, please. And some water. *(Turning back to Rachel.)* Oh no, you're crying again.

RACHEL. I miss Dean. *(Rachel puts her head back on the table.)*

ZELDA. I know. I know. It gets easier.

RACHEL. You don't know that. You've never been in love.

ZELDA. I've heard it does. From trustworthy people. *(Zelda again reaches out a hand to touch Rachel's head, and, again, she pulls it away.)* Has this happened before?

RACHEL. *(Into the table.)* Yes.

ZELDA. You get panic attacks?

RACHEL. Sometimes.

ZELDA. What does it feel like?

RACHEL. One moment I'm fine and the next, my throat starts closing up and my heart beats like crazy and I can't make it stop. *(Zelda looks at Rachel, sadly.)*

ZELDA. What happened to make this generation so afraid?

RACHEL. Oh, I don't know, our parents? *(Beat. Zelda looks up at the bar.)*

ZELDA. *(Re: the popcorn.)* Ah. Splendid. *(Zelda gets up and returns with two big bowls of popcorn. She sets one down in front of Rachel and one in front of herself. The women eat popcorn in silence.)* Rachel, about my —

RACHEL. So, you and Henry Mortimer. How long did that last? *(Beat. Zelda clears her throat.)*

ZELDA. On-and-off again for most of my graduate and post-doc work.

RACHEL. Then, what happened?

ZELDA. Nothing. We drifted apart.

RACHEL. Why did you leave Columbia?

ZELDA. I got a grant. *(Beat. Another penny drops.)*

RACHEL. I happened.

ZELDA. That wasn't it.

RACHEL. Of course. It's so obvious. You got pregnant. He was probably married. So you had to disappear. *(Beat.)*

ZELDA. *(Surprised.)* That's your theory?

RACHEL. Am I right?

ZELDA. He *was* married.

RACHEL. I knew it. Did he ask you to have an abortion?

ZELDA. No.

RACHEL. Did he kick you out of the program?

ZELDA. No.

RACHEL. Well, what did he do when you told him?

ZELDA. I never told him. *(Beat.)*

RACHEL. *(Surprised.)* You never told him?

ZELDA. No. I got a grant to study the Hadza. So I left. *(Beat. Rachel stares at her.)*

RACHEL. Are you insane?

ZELDA. What do you mean?

RACHEL. You just decided to go to Tanzania. Pregnant.

ZELDA. Why not.

RACHEL. What if something had gone wrong? And you were stuck in the bush with savages?

ZELDA. We don't say "savages," Rachel. We say "evolutionarily-challenged." *(Zelda smiles at her own joke.)*

RACHEL. I'm serious.

ZELDA. I know. You're always serious. *(Silence.)*

RACHEL. What was it like?

ZELDA. They were very kind to me. Shared their water, their honey, their monkey meat.

RACHEL. You ate monkey meat?

ZELDA. Occasionally.

RACHEL. During my gestation?

ZELDA. Only during your first trimester.

RACHEL. Their genetic code is only a few chromosomes off of ours! No wonder I'm such a disaster.

ZELDA. You're not a disaster.

RACHEL. Yes, I am.

ZELDA. I don't think so.

RACHEL. You're not allowed to think so. You're my mother. *(Beat. Zelda is touched.)*

ZELDA. Even if I weren't. Even if I were just another scientist who attended the NOORB conference, I would think you were a strong young mind with a bright future ahead of you.

RACHEL. That's because you went to the bathroom. Every other scientist at that conference thinks I'm an embarrassment. I can't go back to my lab —

ZELDA. *(Alarmed.)* Why not?

RACHEL. I can't face it. Dean will be there. My career is ruined.

ZELDA. Your career is not ruined.

RACHEL. I suppose I could teach —

ZELDA. *(Confused.)* Teach?

RACHEL. At a high school level —

ZELDA. Rachel —

RACHEL. Or maybe I should go back to school for something else. Medicine maybe. I could be a doctor. I already know most of the science —

ZELDA. RACHEL! You are going back to the lab.

RACHEL. No, I can't.

ZELDA. Are you crazy?

RACHEL. Everybody is going to laugh at me.

ZELDA. So what if they laugh at you?

RACHEL. It's a horrible feeling.

ZELDA. Of course it is. And you have those horrible feelings — you experience that failure — that sense of the embarrassment — of loss — so that when you come back again, swinging hard, and you do finally knock some of the pins down — or maybe even, one day, all of the pins — you will know it was no accident. Rachel, your youth … your horrible, burdensome, terrifying youth will not last forever. I promise you. It will be over the moment you've finally started to enjoy it. And after that, everything goes. Your eggs first. Your body next. Your mind, *even your mind*, will one day leave you. We end our lives like hollow shells along the beach, rattling around as the water wears us white, indistinguishable from our neighbors. *That* is what you have to look forward to. You want to beat them? The ones who've laughed at you? I'll tell you how. It's very simple, really. Just survive. Go back to your laboratory. Put your face back to the microscope, keep your eyes open, and stay there for another forty years. I promise you, if you do that — you will win your war.

RACHEL. What about the times that I can't be in the lab? Because they've locked it? Because it's, say, Christmas? I've always spent the holidays with Dean's family. What am I supposed to do now? *(Beat.)*

ZELDA. Come with me.

RACHEL. *(Confused.)* You?

ZELDA. I go up to this little inn in New Hampshire. It usually snows too hard to do much of anything, but I can show you how to tap a maple tree. *(Beat. Rachel stares at her.)* You should come.

RACHEL. To spend Christmas with you. Just the two of us. *(Beat.)* I'll think about it.

ZELDA. *(Excited.)* In the town, there are the most charming little antique stores. I've always wanted to spend an afternoon looking through them. I don't know why I haven't. Antiquing just seemed like something people do together. Maybe we could find you an old Singer sewing machine table. Have you ever seen one of those? I had one as a girl. It was the perfect size for a child's desk. *(Rachel is getting increasingly uncomfortable.)*

RACHEL. Yeah, maybe.

ZELDA. We don't have to. Not everyone likes antiques.

RACHEL. No, if I come, we should go.

ZELDA. "If" you come.

RACHEL. I was just thinking … it wouldn't be so hard to get a key to the lab over Christmas. I bet they'd leave the power on if I ask them to. I know that's probably not considered good for my psyche or whatever, but it's just … I mean, if your friend Marie is right, and the anti-pathogen theory of menstruation is wrong, well then, I don't really have time to take a holiday. I've got to get back to the lab and figure something else out.

ZELDA. You have plenty of time.

RACHEL. Not really. You had the Grandmother Hypothesis by the time you were my age, didn't you? Isn't that why you gave me up?

ZELDA. What?

RACHEL. You went into the bush. You saw how those primitive women passed their kids around, to their mothers, their sisters, it takes a village, blah, blah, blah. You had a breakthrough. And you knew it was good. Good enough to carry you home. Good enough to get you tenure. But you also knew that it would be hard to take seriously a single woman who walked out of the bush with a radical hypothesis and a fatherless child. And since you never really wanted the baby to begin with —

ZELDA. Stop it.

RACHEL. What's wrong?

ZELDA. You don't have the slightest idea what you're talking about.

RACHEL. *(Angry.)* Maybe not. But spare me your *Little House on the Prairie* fantasies. Antiquing? You gave up your baby. I just want to work through Christmas. *(Beat.)*

ZELDA. Then I'll come to you. I have an old friend with an apartment in the city. She's on sabbatical; I'm sure I could stay there.

RACHEL. Why?

ZELDA. Why not? I'll make us a goose. We're family, Rachel. *(Rachel has something she needs to say. She takes a deep breath.)*

RACHEL. You made a choice, Zelda. I understand why you did it, but you can't take it back. You are the woman who gave birth to me. You are not my mother. I don't have to hold your hand while you die. *(Silence.)* I've already buried two parents.

ZELDA. I understand.

RACHEL. I'm sorry.

ZELDA. Don't be. You're protecting yourself. Don't ever apologize for that. *(Silence. Neither woman knows what to say.)*

RACHEL. Do you have anyone?

ZELDA. What do you mean?

RACHEL. Who can ... be with you?

ZELDA. Oh. Of course. I have friends.

RACHEL. What about Henry?

ZELDA. *(Surprised.)* Henry?

RACHEL. Are you still in touch?

ZELDA. I haven't spoken to Henry since ... I hear about him from time to time, of course. Mostly from my graduate students who have moved on to post-docs in his lab ... He sounds happy. *(Beat. There's something still bothering Rachel.)*

RACHEL. Here's what I can't figure out. In science, every phenomenon is explainable from two perspectives. The how and the why. I understand how I happened. I still don't understand why. *(Beat. Zelda doesn't respond.)* Why didn't you just have an abortion?

ZELDA. I didn't want to.

RACHEL. Are you religious?

ZELDA. No, I'm Darwinian. *(Silence. Something suddenly occurs to Rachel.)*

RACHEL. I just thought of a counter-hypothesis.

ZELDA. Tell me.

RACHEL. What if you loved Henry? Really loved him? And you wanted to have a child with him. Because that's what women do. We fall in love with men and we think, "Wouldn't it be nice to have his babies?" What if you got pregnant on purpose? Because you thought that was the way to get him to finally leave his wife. But he wouldn't. So you fled. All the way to Africa.

ZELDA. That's quite an accusation.

RACHEL. Why? What's so horrible about it? Why can't you just admit it, Zelda? *You fell in love.* For one moment in your life, you wanted something beyond your illustrious career. That's why I was born. *(Beat.)* Am I right?

ZELDA. *(Clears her throat.)* You're a good scientist, sweetheart. You're crazy as a loon, but you're fearless, so you'll go far.

RACHEL. *(Annoyed.)* Am I right?

ZELDA. Henry had already left his wife for me. We were living together when I went to Tanzania. *(Beat.)*

RACHEL. Then I don't understand. What happened?

ZELDA. I had an idea, Rachel. A good one. But its implications meant the refutation of everything my lover believed. The principles on which he had built his entire career. *(Beat.)* I could publish my hypothesis. Or I could bury it. And go on with Henry. Probably grow old with him. *(Beat.)* I chose to publish it anyway.

RACHEL. Why?

ZELDA. How could I not? *(Silence.)*

RACHEL. Weren't you scared?

ZELDA. Of what?

RACHEL. Being alone? *(Zelda shrugs.)*

ZELDA. "Safe among the solid rock the ugly houses stand: // Come see my shining palace built upon the sand."

RACHEL. Edna again? *(Zelda nods.)* Did your oncologist really give you that plaque? The one in your office?

ZELDA. No.

RACHEL. So who's M?

ZELDA. Mortimer.

RACHEL. Henry.

ZELDA. Yes.

RACHEL. When?

ZELDA. Before you were born. *(Silence.)*

RACHEL. It sounds like he was crazy about you. *(Beat.)*

ZELDA. I was crazy about him too. *(Silence. And from the silence, comes the question of the play.)*

RACHEL. So … was it worth it? *(Zelda thinks. For a long time.)*

ZELDA. Some days, yes. Some days, no. *(Silence.)*

RACHEL. Why didn't you keep me? *(Zelda looks at Rachel.)*
ZELDA. I wish I had. *(Rachel puts her head back down on the table. She doesn't know what to believe anymore. Zelda reaches out and, very tentatively, strokes Rachel's hair. Just once. More silence.)*
RACHEL. Can I ask you something else?
ZELDA. Anything.
RACHEL. Is my whole life going to be this hard?
ZELDA. It depends what you do with it. It will either be hard or boring. You get to pick.
RACHEL. What do I do now?
ZELDA. Get back to your lab.
RACHEL. And work on what?
ZELDA. Your hypothesis.
RACHEL. It's broken.
ZELDA. No, Rachel. It isn't complete.
RACHEL. I don't know how to fix it. *(Beat.)*
ZELDA. Prehistoric women were continually pregnant. So they didn't bleed. How then did their bodies protect themselves from the toxicity of sperm?
RACHEL. I don't know.
ZELDA. Well, let's think about it. What protects the uterus from sperm?
RACHEL. Menstruation.
ZELDA. Anything else? *(Rachel just stares at her.)* What separates the uterus from the vaginal canal?
RACHEL. The cervix.
ZELDA. And what happens to the cervix during pregnancy? *(Again, Rachel doesn't know.)* It thickens. Seals itself off with a chemically hostile coat of mucus. That coat lessens and becomes permeable again after the second trimest —
RACHEL. But by that time, a female would be so obviously pregnant, she wouldn't be attractive to a male. *(Zelda nods. Waits.) Shit.*
ZELDA. There's more. Women have sex after menopause. How then do their bodies continue to protect themselves?
RACHEL. The cervix?
ZELDA. Yes.
RACHEL. It thickens after menopause?
ZELDA. Look it up. *(Rachel stares at Zelda.)*
RACHEL. Fuck. Me. So they can both be right?
ZELDA. They can both be right.

RACHEL. *(Overwhelmed.)* Thank you.

ZELDA. You're welcome. *(Silence.)*

RACHEL. I should really be going. I wanted to catch the last train back to Penn Station. *(Zelda nods.)*

ZELDA. I'll get the check.

RACHEL. I already paid for the drinks.

ZELDA. What about the popcorn?

RACHEL. It's free.

ZELDA. Free? *(Zelda looks around.)* I'll have to remember this place. *(They both stand. They don't know what to do. Zelda puts out her hand to shake. Rachel throws her arms around her mother. They separate. Rachel heads towards the door. Zelda sits down again, slowly. Rachel turns back.)*

RACHEL. *(Alarmed.)* Are you okay?

ZELDA. Fine.

RACHEL. Are you coming? *(Zelda shakes her head.)*

ZELDA. I'm going to stay here a bit. *(Beat. Rachel looks at Zelda.)*

RACHEL. *(Gently.)* Want to hear something funny?

ZELDA. Sure.

RACHEL. They told me I was adopted when I was five. And for years after that, whenever I got angry at my mother, I would say: "You're not my real mother. My real mother is a queen and I'm a princess." *(Zelda starts to cry.)*

ZELDA. That is funny. *(Rachel crosses back to the table. Sits down opposite Zelda. Takes her hands.)*

RACHEL. Some days, I'm so sad, I wish I were dead.

ZELDA. I have those days too.

RACHEL. I don't know what to do about them.

ZELDA. Ride them through.

End of Play

PROPERTY LIST

Unbound manuscript
Open books
Champagne
2 paper cups
Wooden plaque with Edna St. Vincent Millay quotation
Box of tissues
Pack of cigarettes
Lighter
Glass of bourbon
Glass of white wine
2 bowls of popcorn

SOUND EFFECTS

Desk phone ringing
Cell phone ringing

NEW PLAYS

★ **MOTHERS AND SONS by Terrence McNally.** At turns funny and powerful, MOTHERS AND SONS portrays a woman who pays an unexpected visit to the New York apartment of her late son's partner, who is now married to another man and has a young son. Challenged to face how society has changed around her, generations collide as she revisits the past and begins to see the life her son might have led. "A resonant elegy for a ravaged generation." –NY Times. "A moving reflection on a changed America." –Chicago Tribune. [2M, 1W, 1 boy] ISBN: 978-0-8222-3183-7

★ **THE HEIR APPARENT by David Ives, adapted from Le Légataire Universel by Jean-François Regnard.** Paris, 1708. Eraste, a worthy though penniless young man, is in love with the fair Isabelle, but her forbidding mother, Madame Argante, will only let the two marry if Eraste can show he will inherit the estate of his rich but miserly Uncle Geronte. Unfortunately, old Geronte has also fallen for the fair Isabelle, and plans to marry her this very day and leave her everything in his will—separating the two young lovers forever. Eraste's wily servant Crispin jumps in, getting a couple of meddling relatives disinherited by impersonating them (one, a brash American, the other a French female country cousin)—only to have the old man kick off before his will is made! In a brilliant stroke, Crispin then impersonates the old man, dictating a will favorable to his master (and Crispin himself, of course)—only to find that rich Uncle Geronte isn't dead at all and is more than ever ready to marry Isabelle! The multiple strands of the plot are unraveled to great comic effect in the streaming rhyming couplets of French classical comedy, and everyone lives happily, and richly, ever after. [4M, 3W] ISBN: 978-0-8222-2808-0

★ **HANDLE WITH CARE by Jason Odell Williams.** Circumstances both hilarious and tragic bring together a young Israeli woman, who has little command of English, and a young American man, who has little command of romance. Is their inevitable love an accident…or is it destiny, generations in the making? "A hilarious and heart-warming romantic comedy." –NY Times. "Hilariously funny! Utterly charming, fearlessly adorable and a tiny bit magical." –Naples News. [2M, 2W] ISBN: 978-0-8222-3138-7

★ **LAST GAS by John Cariani.** Nat Paradis is a Red Sox-loving part-time dad who manages Paradis' Last Convenient Store, the last convenient place to get gas—or anything—before the Canadian border to the north and the North Maine Woods to the west. When an old flame returns to town, Nat gets a chance to rekindle a romance he gave up on years ago. But sparks fly as he's forced to choose between new love and old. "Peppered with poignant characters [and] sharp writing." –Portland Phoenix. "Very funny and surprisingly thought-provoking." –Portland Press Herald. [4M, 3W] ISBN: 978-0-8222-3232-2

DRAMATISTS PLAY SERVICE, INC.
440 Park Avenue South, New York, NY 10016 212-683-8960 Fax 212-213-1539
postmaster@dramatists.com www.dramatists.com

NEW PLAYS

★ **ACT ONE by James Lapine.** Growing up in an impoverished Bronx family and forced to drop out of school at age thirteen, Moss Hart dreamed of joining the glamorous world of the theater. Hart's famous memoir *Act One* plots his unlikely collaboration with the legendary playwright George S. Kaufman and his arrival on Broadway. Tony Award-winning writer and director James Lapine has adapted Act One for the stage, creating a funny, heartbreaking and suspenseful celebration of a playwright and his work. "…brims contagiously with the ineffable, irrational and irrefutable passion for that endangered religion called the Theater." –NY Times. "…wrought with abundant skill and empathy." –Time Out. [8M, 4W] ISBN: 978-0-8222-3217-9

★ **THE VEIL by Conor McPherson.** May 1822, rural Ireland. The defrocked Reverend Berkeley arrives at the crumbling former glory of Mount Prospect House to accompany a young woman to England. Seventeen-year-old Hannah is to be married off to a marquis in order to resolve the debts of her mother's estate. However, compelled by the strange voices that haunt his beautiful young charge and a fascination with the psychic current that pervades the house, Berkeley proposes a séance, the consequences of which are catastrophic. "…an effective mixture of dark comedy and suspense." –Telegraph (London). "A cracking fireside tale of haunting and decay." –Times (London). [3M, 5W] ISBN: 978-0-8222-3313-8

★ **AN OCTOROON by Branden Jacobs-Jenkins. Winner of the 2014 OBIE Award for Best New American Play.** Judge Peyton is dead and his plantation Terrebonne is in financial ruins. Peyton's handsome nephew George arrives as heir apparent and quickly falls in love with Zoe, a beautiful octoroon. But the evil overseer M'Closky has other plans—for both Terrebonne and Zoe. In 1859, a famous Irishman wrote this play about slavery in America. Now an American tries to write his own. "AN OCTOROON invites us to laugh loudly and easily at how naïve the old stereotypes now seem, until nothing seems funny at all." –NY Times [10M, 5W] ISBN: 978-0-8222-3226-1

★ **IVANOV translated and adapted by Curt Columbus.** In this fascinating early work by Anton Chekhov, we see the union of humor and pathos that would become his trademark. A restless man, Nicholai Ivanov struggles to dig himself out of debt and out of provincial boredom. When the local doctor, Lvov, informs Ivanov that his wife Anna is dying and accuses him of worsening her condition with his foul moods, Ivanov is sent into a downward spiral of depression and ennui. He soon finds himself drawn to a beautiful young woman, Sasha, full of hope and energy. Finding himself stuck between a romantic young mistress and his ailing wife, Ivanov falls deeper into crisis, heading toward inevitable tragedy. [8M, 8W] ISBN: 978-0-8222-3155-4

DRAMATISTS PLAY SERVICE, INC.
440 Park Avenue South, New York, NY 10016 212-683-8960 Fax 212-213-1539
postmaster@dramatists.com www.dramatists.com

NEW PLAYS

★ **I'LL EAT YOU LAST: A CHAT WITH SUE MENGERS by John Logan.** For more than 20 years, Sue Mengers' clients were the biggest names in show business: Barbra Streisand, Faye Dunaway, Burt Reynolds, Ali MacGraw, Gene Hackman, Cher, Candice Bergen, Ryan O'Neal, Nick Nolte, Mike Nichols, Gore Vidal, Bob Fosse…If her clients were the talk of the town, she was the town, and her dinner parties were the envy of Hollywood. Now, you're invited into her glamorous Beverly Hills home for an evening of dish, dirty secrets and all the inside showbiz details only Sue can tell you. "A delectable soufflé of a solo show…thanks to the buoyant, witty writing of Mr. Logan" –NY Times. "80 irresistible minutes of primo tinseltown dish from a certified master chef." –Hollywood Reporter. [1W] ISBN: 978-0-8222-3079-3

★ **PUNK ROCK by Simon Stephens.** In a private school outside of Manchester, England, a group of highly-articulate seventeen-year-olds flirt and posture their way through the day while preparing for their A-Level mock exams. With hormones raging and minimal adult supervision, the students must prepare for their future — and survive the savagery of high school. Inspired by playwright Simon Stephens' own experiences as a teacher, PUNK ROCK is an honest and unnerving chronicle of contemporary adolescence. "[A] tender, ferocious and frightning play." –NY Times. "[A] muscular little play that starts out funny and ferocious then reveals its compassion by degrees." –Hollywood Reporter. [5M, 3W] ISBN: 978-0-8222-3288-9

★ **THE COUNTRY HOUSE by Donald Margulies.** A brood of famous and longing-to-be-famous creative artists have gathered at their summer home during the Williamstown Theatre Festival. When the weekend takes an unexpected turn, everyone is forced to improvise, inciting a series of simmering jealousies, romantic outbursts, and passionate soul-searching. Both witty and compelling, THE COUNTRY HOUSE provides a piercing look at a family of performers coming to terms with the roles they play in each other's lives. "A valentine to the artists of the stage." –NY Times. "Remarkably candid and funny." –Variety. [3M, 3W] ISBN: 978-0-8222-3274-2

★ **OUR LADY OF KIBEHO by Katori Hall.** Based on real events, OUR LADY OF KIBEHO is an exploration of faith, doubt, and the power and consequences of both. In 1981, a village girl in Rwanda claims to see the Virgin Mary. Ostracized by her schoolmates and labeled disturbed, everyone refuses to believe, until impossible happenings appear again and again. Skepticism gives way to fear, and then to belief, causing upheaval in the school community and beyond. "Transfixing." –NY Times. "Hall's passionate play renews belief in what theater can do." –Time Out [7M, 8W, 1 boy] ISBN: 978-0-8222-3301-5

DRAMATISTS PLAY SERVICE, INC.
440 Park Avenue South, New York, NY 10016 212-683-8960 Fax 212-213-1539
postmaster@dramatists.com www.dramatists.com

NEW PLAYS

★ **AGES OF THE MOON by Sam Shepard.** Byron and Ames are old friends, reunited by mutual desperation. Over bourbon on ice, they sit, reflect and bicker until fifty years of love, friendship and rivalry are put to the test at the barrel of a gun. "A poignant and honest continuation of themes that have always been present in the work of one of this country's most important dramatists, here reconsidered in the light and shadow of time passed." –NY Times. "Finely wrought...as enjoyable and enlightening as a night spent stargazing." –Talkin' Broadway. [2M] ISBN: 978-0-8222-2462-4

★ **ALL THE WAY by Robert Schenkkan. Winner of the 2014 Tony Award for Best Play.** November, 1963. An assassin's bullet catapults Lyndon Baines Johnson into the presidency. A Shakespearean figure of towering ambition and appetite, this charismatic, conflicted Texan hurls himself into the passage of the Civil Rights Act—a tinderbox issue emblematic of a divided America—even as he campaigns for re-election in his own right, and the recognition he so desperately wants. In Pulitzer Prize and Tony Award–winning Robert Schenkkan's vivid dramatization of LBJ's first year in office, means versus ends plays out on the precipice of modern America. ALL THE WAY is a searing, enthralling exploration of the morality of power. It's not personal, it's just politics. "...action-packed, thoroughly gripping... jaw-dropping political drama." –Variety. "A theatrical coup...nonstop action. The suspense of a first-class thriller." –NY1. [17M, 3W] ISBN: 978-0-8222-3181-3

★ **CHOIR BOY by Tarell Alvin McCraney.** The Charles R. Drew Prep School for Boys is dedicated to the creation of strong, ethical black men. Pharus wants nothing more than to take his rightful place as leader of the school's legendary gospel choir. Can he find his way inside the hallowed halls of this institution if he sings in his own key? "[An] affecting and honest portrait...of a gay youth tentatively beginning to find the courage to let the truth about himself become known." –NY Times. "In his stirring and stylishly told drama, Tarell Alvin McCraney cannily explores race and sexuality and the graces and gravity of history." –NY Daily News. [7M] ISBN: 978-0-8222-3116-5

★ **THE ELECTRIC BABY by Stefanie Zadravec.** When Helen causes a car accident that kills a young man, a group of fractured souls cross paths and connect around a mysterious dying baby who glows like the moon. Folk tales and folklore weave throughout this magical story of sad endings, strange beginnings and the unlikely people that get you from one place to the next. "The imperceptible magic that pervades human existence and the power of myth to assuage sorrow are invoked by the playwright as she entwines the lives of strangers in THE ELECTRIC BABY, a touching drama." –NY Times. "As dazzling as the dialogue is dreamful." –Pittsburgh City Paper. [3M, 3W] ISBN: 978-0-8222-3011-3

DRAMATISTS PLAY SERVICE, INC.
440 Park Avenue South, New York, NY 10016 212-683-8960 Fax 212-213-1539
postmaster@dramatists.com www.dramatists.com